Illustrations by Angela Mitson Written by Giles Reed

PUBLISHED BY STUDIO PUBLICATIONS (IPSWICH) LIMITED
32 PRINCES STREET, IPSWICH, SUFFOLK, ENGLAND.

Rory Rhubarb is one of the Munch Bunch. He lives in a shortbread tin.

And because Rory comes from Scotland, he has painted his house with tartan paint.

He does the strangest things at the strangest times. His friends think he is eccentric.

It was three o'clock in the morning. It was time for Rory to get up.

He always gets up at very strange times.

As you can see, Rory sleeps in a very strange way.

Even his alarm clock is different.

Rory quickly got dressed and found his bagpipes.

And then he went outside and started to play them.

Because the bagpipes had not been tuned, they made a horrible screeching noise.

As it was still only ten past three in the morning, the Munch Bunch were still fast asleep.

But the sound of Rory's bagpipes soon woke them up.

Pete Pepper was very angry, and Olly Onion was crying – as usual.

Merv Marrow led the way to Rory's house to see what all the noise was about.

Rory explained that it was the start of the haggis season, and that he was playing the Haggis Hunt tune.

The others didn't know what a haggis was.

"It's a Scottish creature that runs round the side of a hill all day," explained Rory. "It has two short legs and two long legs, and you have to get up early to catch one."

Olly Onion and the others thought a Haggis Hunt sounded like good fun.

So they decided to go to the hills to try to catch one.

Rory Rhubarb chuckled to himself as his friends started the hunt.

Well, we all know a haggis is not really an animal at all, don't we?

Rory finished playing his tune on the bagpipes and went home to have a nice porridge sandwich for his supper.

He always had his supper at breakfast time.

And he always had his porridge in a sandwich.

Then he made himself a cup of tea.

His teapot is a watering-can, and his cups are Scottish sporrans. Rory always drinks his tea from sporrans.

And he always has three cups at a time!

Suddenly, Rory noticed it was raining.

"Great," he said to himself. "I'll just do a spot of rain-bathing."

So he quickly grabbed his deck-chair and ran outside. And he sat down to enjoy the rain.

When he had finished rain-bathing, Rory decided to water his flowers.

He always uses a teapot instead of a watering-can to water his flowers.

He could not help chuckling to himself when he thought about the others still out on the Haggis Hunt.

When the rain stopped, Rory decided to take Nessie, his pet snail, for a walk.

And because the sun was out, Rory took his umbrella.

As soon as Rory got home, he collected together all the ingredients for making a haggis.

And then he mixed them all up in his bath-tub.

Rory decided that when his friends returned from the Haggis Hunt, they should have some real haggis for their tea.

Lucy Lemon and the others were very hot, very tired and very dirty when they returned from the Haggis Hunt.

And they were very ANGRY with Rory.

"The haggis must have heard you coming and hidden," said Rory. "But never mind, I caught some this morning. So I hope you will join me for breakfast tonight."

Rory's haggis was delicious. The Munch Bunch ate lots and lots of it.

"How come you caught so many, but we couldn't even catch one?" asked Lucy.

"I lured them here with my bagpipes," replied Rory, trying not to smile.

When they had finished their meal, Rory tuned his bagpipes and started to play some Scottish music.

They danced the Scottish sword dances and highland flings.

Everyone had great fun.

When everyone had gone home, Rory was still chuckling to himself about the "Wild Haggis Chase" he had sent his friends on.

Well, he couldn't give an old Scottish secret away, could he?